A.S. DELEEUW

A Quick Guide to Nutrition 4 Better Mental Health

Contents

1 Introduction   1

2 Nutrients for Optimal Mental Health   4

3 Balancing Blood Sugar for Mental Health   47

4 The Connection between Gut Health and Mental Health   73

5 Meals & Snacks for Better Mental Health   89

6 Conclusion   94

7 Resources   95

8 Appendix   97

About the Author   100

1

Introduction

Welcome

Welcome to A Quick *Guide to Nutrition for Better Mental Health*! I'm beyond excited to share the information in this book for so many reasons. I'm not going to list them out, but I can sum it up by saying that the contents of this guide can change your life if you're struggling with depression and/or anxiety. And I can say this with confidence because the knowledge I'm about to share has improved my own life immeasurably. I no longer struggle with the debilitating symptoms of depression and anxiety simply because I've learned how to eat for better mental health. Now it's your turn!

What to Expect

In this book, you will learn about the essential nutrients your body needs to prevent and alleviate symptoms of depression and anxiety. Too many of us aren't getting these nutrients for a whole slew of reasons. I'll explain that in more detail in the "Nutrients for Optimal Mental Health" chapter of this guide.

You'll also learn about the importance of balancing your blood sugar and get tips for doing just that. Many people don't know this, but blood sugar plays a starring role in both the development of and healing from depression and anxiety. Essentially, stable blood sugar leads to stable moods and balanced energy levels – neither of which you're likely experiencing if you struggle with these mental health conditions.

From there, you'll gain an understanding of the gut-brain connection and how an unbalanced gut or microbiome can wreak havoc on your mental health. You'll also learn how you can heal your own gut so that you can heal from depression and/or anxiety.

Finally, you'll get some tips for throwing together easy meals and snacks that:

- Are full of the nutrients you need,
- Will balance your blood sugar, and
- Can heal your gut.

Sounds pretty amazing, right? Yep. And that's because it is

A Little about Me

Hi there! I'm Anne, and I feel passionate about this topic because I've been in your shoes. I've had depression. I've experienced anxiety. And in order to deal, I've cycled on and off of anti-depressant medications and in and out of therapy. The results of these efforts were always a little "meh" at best until I learned how to eat in a way that would truly help me heal from depression and anxiety. And now I just can't wait to share what I've learned with you. I even dropped everything mid-life to earn an MS in Nutrition Education. That's how strongly I feel about the power of foods to help you heal. And I know that the information in this book can help you overcome your symptoms of depression and/or anxiety.

So, let's get you started!

2

Nutrients for Optimal Mental Health

Introduction

Scientific research has concluded that both micro- and macronutrients from a balanced diet are essential for healthy brain function and good mental health. (Muscaritoli, 2021). Specifically, vitamins, minerals, fatty acids, and amino acids help the brain function. And I don't want to get into a lot of fancy scientific jargon here. But basically, it comes down to this: What we eat affects our brain health. Diet is a modifiable variable in the presence or absence of good mental health (Adan et al., 2019) And our brain health is the most significant factor in whether we develop depression and anxiety*and*whether we can heal from depression and anxiety.

Here's the thing: most of us are not getting the nutrients that we need to have a healthy brain. There are different reasons for this. In her book*The Mood Cure*, Julia Ross points out that we're in the midst of a junk food epidemic, and, as a result, we are undernourished as never before (Ross, The Mood Cure, p. 84). I don't think anyone can argue with this. And Ross goes on to say that when a person is malnourished, their mood deteriorates even before their physical health declines (Ross, The Mood Cure, p. 122).

So, those of us eating the Standard American Diet (a.k.a "SAD," – how appropriate) are most likely not giving our brains the nutrients they need in o to fend off or heal from depression and anxiety. Now I understand that not everyone who eats the SAD has depression and anxiety. But those of us who are genetically predisposed to these mental health disorders and who have been exposed to environmental factors associated with depression and anxiety simply can't get by on the typical American diet full of carbs, refined sugars, and unhealthy saturated fats. That's because this type of diet doesn't have the vitamins, minerals, essential fatty acids, and amino acids that our minds (and bodies) need to thrive.

And even when you're eating healthfully and getting better nutrition than the SAD provides, you may not be getting enough of certain nutrients. That's because nutrients are complex, and some people even have genetic variants that prevent them from absorbing or processing different nutrients that are vital to health – including mental health. Additionally, the reference daily intakes or RDIs established by the Food and Drug Administration (FDA) are on the low side at best.

And there's more. You may have heard that stress plays a significant role in the development of depression and anxiety. It's the truth! There are many reasons for this. But one reason is that stress messes with your ability to absorb and maintain nutrients. In *The Mood Cure*, Ross points out that after just one stress-filled week, your supplies of the vitamins and minerals that help prevent the development of depression can drop by as much as 30-40%.

When you're stressed, your adrenals use up about 90 percent of your *vitamin C* intake. And you need vitamin C to fight depression and anxiety. Additionally, the adrenal glands require a constant supply of *B vitamins* when you're stressed. So, it can become really difficult to get enough of these. Also, your adrenal glands quickly us up your stores of *calcium, magnesium,* and *vitamin D* during times of stress. And your adrenals need a healthy supply of both vitamin D and *omega-3 fatty acids* to make stress-fighting adrenaline and norepinephrine (Ross, The Mood Cure, p. 94).

Finally, the SAD diet doesn't provide our bodies with the nutrients they need to fight off inflammation, which is another factor that plays into the development of mental health disorders like depression and anxiety. Studies have shown that nutrients like folic acid, magnesium, and the EPA and DHA found in omega fatty acids help control inflammation to preserve brain function and optimal mental health (Muscaritoli, 2021).

Furthermore, food processing systems strip much of the nutritional value from the foods we eat. Even unprocessed foods such as fruits and vegetables don't always contain the vitamins and minerals that they should. That's because much of the soil these foods are grown in has become depleted of these nutrients.

So, when you're struggling with depression and anxiety, you need to put in some extra effort to get the nutrients that you need. I know this isn't always an easy task. But trust me, it's worth it! In her book *This is Your Brain on Food*, Uma Naidoo, MD, says that she sees most patients improve drastically with nutritional therapy within 6 months. (Naidoo, This Is Your Brain on Food, p. 76). The changes are incremental. Some of you will see improvements sooner than others. Naidoo notes that some people see results in as little as 6 weeks or even 28 days. But for most of you, it will take a little more time to see the benefits. Don't give up!

With all that said, I'd like to talk a little more about the nutrients you need for optimal mental health.

Vitamins

B Vitamins

There are so, so many reasons that you need your Bs for optimal mental health! It's almost hard for me to know where to begin on this one. But here goes…

For starters (and the most straightforward reason), **B vitamins are necessary for producing neurotransmitters such as serotonin and dopamine**, which are essential for mood regulation. And B12, B6, and folate are especially important for preventing and managing depression.

Additionally, **you need B vitamins to metabolize sugar**!!!!! *And unbalanced blood sugar is associated with a whole slew of unwanted health conditions – including depression and anxiety.* We'll talk a lot more about blood sugar in the next chapter.

And you don't need to worry too much about overdoing vitamin B supplements because B vitamins are water soluble. But as always, check with your doctor before taking any supplements. And start with lower doses to see how well you tolerate them. Then build from there.

With that said, here is a list of the B vitamins and some of the specifics about why you need them:

B1 – Thiamine.

Vitamin B1 or thiamine deficiencies can trigger depression, anxiety, irritability, and insomnia. One specific reason that we need vitamin B1 is that our brains use it to convert glucose or blood sugar into energy. This helps balance our blood sugar. And again, unbalanced blood sugar is commonly associated with depression and anxiety. B1 also helps maintain the nervous system so it can combat symptoms associated with stress. And people who have healthy responses to stress are less prone to developing depression, anxiety and insomnia. You get the idea.

Salmon, sunflower seeds, peas, meats, lentils, yogurt, and eggs are all good sources of B1.

B2 – Riboflavin.

B2 deficiency has been linked to depression and anxiety. This vitamin supports cellular function, provides the body with energy, and facilitates the production of hormones from the adrenal glands – in other words, the stress hormones. So, you may have a hard time getting enough of certain B vitamins, such as B2, when you're under stress.

Eggs, milk, mushrooms, almonds, beef, spinach, yogurt, avocado, salmon, cheese, and chicken are all good sources of B2.

B3 – Niacin.

B3 provides the body with energy, supports the nervous system, and boosts brain function. It's not too surprising then that B3 deficiency is associated with depression and anxiety. In fact, the symptoms of B3 deficiency and of depression and anxiety are similar, including fatigue, depressed mood, insomnia, nervousness, and apprehension.

Chicken, turkey, brown rice, peanuts, and potatoes are all excellent sources of B3.

B6 – Pyridoxine

B6 is a coenzyme needed for converting tryptophan to serotonin and both phenylalanine and tyrosine into norepinephrine. Serotonin and norepinephrine are neurochemicals that play significant roles in mental health. It's not surprising then that B6 deficiency has been linked to depression and anxiety. We will talk more about tryptophan, phenylalanine, and tyrosine later in this chapter.

Spinach, potatoes, sweet potatoes, chickpeas, raisins, sunflower seeds, and bananas are all high in vitamin B6.

B7 – Biotin

Higher levels of biotin intake may lower the incidence of depression. This may be due to the fact that biotin stabilizes blood sugar levels. And again, unbalanced blood sugar is linked to depression.

Peas, lentils, sunflower seeds, carrots, cauliflower, mushrooms, eggs, dairy products, seafood, and whole grains are all great sources of biotin.

B8 - Inositol

B8 or inositol converts into a substance that regulates the action of serotonin within nerve cells. And, as you know, serotonin plays a significant role in both the development and treatment of depression and anxiety.

Beans, grains, and nuts are excellent sources of vitamin B8.

B9 – Folate or Folic Acid

B9 or folate also helps regulate levels of neurotransmitters such as serotonin and dopamine. And so low folate levels may contribute to the development of depression. It's relatively easy to get enough folate in your diet. *However, some people have a genetic irregularity that makes it difficult for them to process and absorb folate.* These people are more susceptible to depression.

Fortified cereals, avocado, beans, asparagus, eggs, bananas, and spinach are all excellent sources of folate.

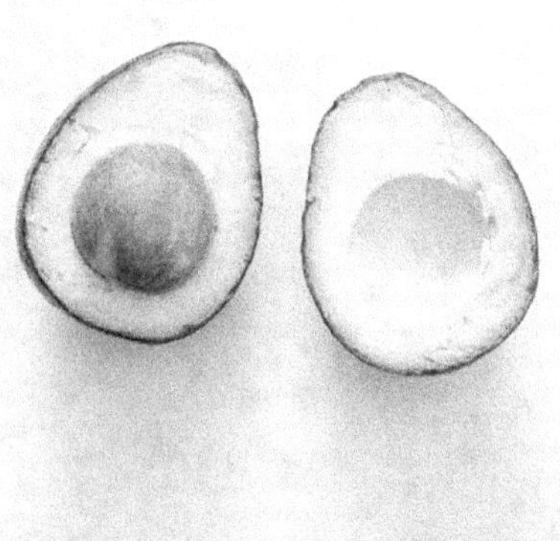

B12 – Cobalamin

Your body uses B12 to form red blood cells. When a person is deficient in this vitamin, they may have an issue with oxygen transport in their body, a condition referred to as pernicious anemia. This condition can lead to mood swings and irritability. B12 has also been linked to the development of serotonin in the brain. Many symptoms of B12 deficiency are the same symptoms of depression, and B12 deficiency is commonly identified as a trigger of depression. And research has shown a very strong correlation between vitamin B12 deficiency and depression (Adan et al., 2019)

Fish, poultry, lean meats, eggs, milk, and fortified breakfast cereals are great sources of B12.

Of note: Vegetarians and vegans are more likely to develop a B12 deficiency because animal products are the best sources of this vitamin. So, if you're vegetarian or vegan, you should definitely consider taking a vitamin B12 supplement.

Vitamin C

Vitamin C concentrations are highest in the brain as opposed to other areas of the body. And you guessed it… this vitamin has been linked to depression, fatigue, and anxiety.

That's because vitamin C is important for converting the aminos tyrosine into dopamine and tryptophan into serotonin. Dopamine and serotonin play a role in mental health. Additionally, vitamin C plays a role in the production of GABA, norepinephrine, and epinephrine, all of which are linked to depression and anxiety. Finally, vitamin C helps manage cortisol levels, which play a role in a person's stress response. And again, stress plays a role in the development of depression and anxiety.

And similar to B vitamins, vitamin C is water soluble. So, your body will excrete what it does not need. However, use some caution in terms of supplemental dosage because too much vitamin C can cause diarrhea.

Citrus fruits, cantaloupe, strawberries, broccoli, cauliflower, brussels sprouts, and red peppers are all good sources of vitamin C.

Vitamin D

Finally, low levels of vitamin D have been linked to depression and anxiety. It's unclear if vitamin D deficiencies cause depression. But people with depression often have low levels of vitamin D in their systems. It could be that depressed people spend less time outdoors, and the best source of vitamin D is sunlight.

Additionally, scientific research has shown that people who took vitamin D supplements of 4,000 IU/day for one month and 2,000 IU/day for 2 months significantly improved the severity of their depression, irritability, fatigue, mood swings, sleep issues, and inability to concentrate (Grajek et al., 2022).

Other sources of vitamin D include salmon, sardines, red meat, and egg yolks.

That wraps up what I have to say about vitamins. And I'd just like to note that research has found that people who eat a lot of fruits and vegetables report higher levels of happiness and overall well-being (Adan et al., 2019). And that makes perfect sense because fruits and veggies are chock-full of a lot of the nutrients that are necessary for optimal mental health.

Minerals

Calcium

The first mineral we need to discuss is calcium. I'm sure you've heard that calcium keeps your bones strong. But the mineral has many other functions in the body as well, even some that – you guessed it - relate to mental health.

Calcium helps suppress the central nervous system and control excitatory brain activity. So, without enough of this vital mineral, your central nervous system suffers, leading to anxiety, depression, and general irritability.

Additionally, calcium helps balance your lactate to pyruvate ratio. When you eat carbs and sugary foods, your blood lactate levels rise. But you don't want to have too much lactate in your body, especially in comparison to the pyruvate we have in our bodies. That's because an imbalance of lactate to pyruvate can lead to the development of depression and anxiety.

Foods rich in calcium include:

- All dairy products, including Milk, Yogurt, Cottage Cheese, and Cheese
- Kefir
- Oranges
- Figs
- Broccoli
- Collard Greens
- Kale
- Bok Choy
- Turnip Greens
- Almonds
- Tofu
- Edamame
- Canned Tomatoes
- Butternut Squash
- Black Beans
- White Beans
- Garbanzo Beans

- Canned Seafood, including Sardines, Salmon, and Shrimp
- Whey Protein Powder
- Soy Milk

Magnesium

In *This Is Your Brain on Food*, Dr. Uma Naidoo says that 68% of Americans don't get enough magnesium (Naidoo, This Is Your Brain on Food, p. 77). And magnesium is a biggie when it comes to depression and anxiety.

In fact, magnesium deficiency is commonly associated with the development of depression. And increasing your magnesium levels through nutrient-dense foods or/or supplements can help mitigate symptoms of depression.

How exactly does magnesium help alleviate symptoms of depression? For one, it helps regulate blood sugar levels. For another, it improves sleep quality. And both blood sugar and sleep quality are linked to depression and anxiety.

Sources of magnesium include:

- Avocados
- Almonds
- Cashews
- Peanuts
- Peanut Butter
- Cooked Black Beans
- Edamame
- Whole grains
- Salmon
- Mackerel

Iron

Iron helps oxygen circulate throughout the body. And guess what, it also helps your body make the neurotransmitters serotonin, dopamine, and epinephrine. Symptoms of depleted blood iron levels are very similar to symptoms of depression and anxiety. These include general weakness, listlessness, exhaustion, lack of appetite, and headaches. Sound familiar? Not too surprisingly then, iron supplementation can help improve symptoms of depression and anxiety.

Good sources of iron include:

- Oysters
- Lean Red Meats
- Pumpkin Seeds
- Cashews
- Dried Apricots
- Raisins
- Sweet Potatoes
- Baked Potatoes

- Broccoli
- Peppers
- Spinach
- Peas
- Chickpeas
- Edamame
- Tofu
- White Beans
- Red Kidney Beans
- White Rice
- Lentils
- Quinoa
- Oats
- Iron Fortified Cereal
- Dark Chocolate

It's important to note that iron absorption increases when taken with vitamin C. So, you could eat a salad with peppers, tomatoes, and lentils or steak to increase iron absorption. Or you could take an iron supplement with a glass of orange juice.

It's also important to note that iron absorption decreases when you are getting more than 1000 mg of calcium each day. So, you need calcium, and it's a great thing. Just keep in mind that the more calcium you get in your diet, the more iron you will need as well.

Manganese

Manganese also plays a role in the development and treatment of depression. That's because manganese helps with the formation of certain amino acids that have been linked to depression.

Manganese is also an important cofactor in enzymes involved in serotonin and norepinephrine synthesis. So, a manganese deficiency may lead to low levels or these neurotransmitters.

Additionally, manganese helps metabolize the B complex vitamins and vitamin C. So, if you're getting enough or your Bs and Cs but aren't getting enough manganese, you won't be getting all the benefits from the B and C vitamins.

Finally, manganese helps stabilize blood sugar. And as you well know by now, balanced blood sugar is essential for those prone to depression and anxiety.

Unfortunately, many people suffer from manganese deficiency. One reason is that much of our soil is now deficient of manganese. So, we don't get enough manganese from the foods grown in that soil.

The best source of manganese are:

- Shellfish, such as Mussels, Oysters, and Clams
- Tofu
- Edamame
- Peas
- Lentils
- Chickpeas
- Lima beans
- Sweet potatoes
- Pineapple
- Spinach
- Hazelnuts
- Pecans
- Peanuts
- Brown rice
- Black pepper
- Black tea

Zinc

Zinc is a micronutrient that's part of many different proteins in your body. Without enough zinc, these proteins can't function properly. And some of these proteins regulate the neurotransmitters linked to depression and anxiety.

Zinc also plays a role in decreasing inflammation in the body, and inflammation has been linked to depression and anxiety as well.

And there's a connection between stress, zinc, and depression. Chronic stress may decrease zinc levels in the body. And, as you may well know, prolonged stress can lead to depression.

A zinc deficiency can increase the severity of depressive symptoms, and taking a zinc supplement with antidepressants can significantly stabilize your mood (Grajek et al., 2022).

Good sources of zinc include:

- Oysters
- Crab
- Shrimp
- Mussels
- Poultry
- Beef
- Pork
- Chickpeas
- Lentils
- Beans
- Hemp Seeds
- Pumpkin Seeds
- Sesame Seeds
- Squash
- Pine Nuts
- Cashews

- Almonds
- Peanuts
- Cheese
- Milk
- Eggs
- Whole Grains
- Potatoes
- Kale
- Green Beans
- Dark Chocolate

Of note: Phytic acid, which is found in wheat bran, can block zinc absorption (Naidoo, This Is Your Brain on Food, p. 78).

Potassium

Once again, chronic stress can lead to the development of depression and anxiety. When stressed, your sympathetic nervous system is active. But you need to switch on your parasympathetic nervous system to calm down and feel relaxed. Potassium plays an important role in regulating the parasympathetic nervous system. Potassium depletion has been linked to depression and anxiety. This may be because a person deficient in potassium has difficulty activating their parasympathetic nervous system to deal with chronic stress.

Good sources of potassium include:

- Sweet Potatoes
- Potatoes
- Bananas
- Avocado
- Mushrooms
- Oranges
- Peas
- Cucumbers
- Dried Apricots
- Oranges
- Yogurt
- Tomatoes
- Salmon
- Spinach
- Watermelon
- Black Beans

- Lentils
- Chickpeas
- Soybeans
- Peanuts
- Butternut Squash
- Swiss Chard
- Beets

Omegas

So, this may surprise you, but your brain runs on fat. That's right. It really needs fat to function properly. In fact, the brain's gray matter is 60 percent essential fatty acids. And essential fatty acids play a starring role in emotional stability and in the prevention and treatment of depression and anxiety.

More specifically, we need omega 3 and omega 6 essential fatty acids (EFAs), which help the brain fire and receive messages through neurotransmitters. Without these essential fatty acids, serotonin and norepinephrine can't send their signals. And the appropriate functioning of serotonin and norepinephrine is vital for good mental health. But that's not all. Low omega-3 levels also affect dopamine, mixing up dopamine signals and leading to depression.

Omega 3s also have anti-inflammatory effects on the brain (Grajek et al., 2022). And again, inflammation is a common marker for the development of mental health disorders. Additionally, omega 3s influence the functioning of the BDNF growth hormone, which also plays a role in the development of mental disease. And the omega 3s play a role in the reuptake of neurotransmitters, which is – you guessed it – a significant factor in the development of depression (Grajek et al., 2022).

In *The Depression Cure*, Stephen Ilardi says: "When brain cells don't have enough omega 3, they have trouble interpreting the messages from serotonin, and they start to misfire. This leads to a massive loss of serotonin function throughout the brain, increasing a person's vulnerability to the sort of out-of-control stress response that triggers the onset of depression" (Ilardi, The Depression Cure, p. 70).

Additionally, essential fatty acids help your brain use the oh-so-necessary B vitamins. So, there's not much point to getting the B vitamins you need if you're not getting the oh-so-vital essential fatty acids.

Most of us are more in need of omega 3s than omega 6s. That's because the Standard American Diet is chock-full of omega 6s. And unfortunately, it's more difficult to get the needed omega 3s. Stephen Ilardi points out that we used to get plenty of omega 3s from meat. Back in the day, livestock animals ate grasses and wild plants full of omega 3s and passed those along to us. Today, however, most livestock are grain-fed and are as omega 3 deficient as we are. It's the same thing for fish. Much of the fish we eat is farm-raised, grain-fed, and deficient in omega 3s. Incidentally, today's skyrocketing rates of depression have corresponded with plummeting rates of omega 3 fatty acids in the Standard American Diet.

Again, we do need both omega 3s and omega 6s, however, the ratio should be 1:1. It's currently 16:1 in favor of omega 6s. Ilardi says common symptoms of imbalanced omega 3 to omega 6 ratio include: (The Depression Cure, p. 82)

- Fatigue
- Poor Concentration
- Sluggishness
- Sinus Congestion
- Carbohydrate Craving
- Dry Skin
- Dry Eyes
- Constipation
- Brittle nails and Hair

I probably don't need to point out that some of these symptoms are the very same as symptoms of depression.

Foods full of healthy fats (aka omega 3s) include:

- Avocados
- Olives
- Almonds
- Macadamia Nuts
- Brazil Nuts
- Hazelnuts
- Peanut Butter
- Pine Nuts
- Pecans
- Pistachios
- Walnuts
- Pumpkin Seeds
- Sesame Seeds
- Sunflower Seeds
- Wheat Germ
- Butter
- Hard Cheese
- Feta cheese
- Cottage Cheese
- Whole Milk Yogurt
- Eggs
- Fish, such as Salmon and Tuna
- Beef
- Chicken

That's all I have about the importance of omega fatty acids. But I dare say it's probably enough to get you thinking about how you're going to incorporate more omega 3s in your diet. So, now I'm going to move on to amino acids.

Aminos

Amino acids are the building blocks of protein. And amino acids and their coenzyme vitamins and minerals initiate the development of neurotransmitters such as serotonin and dopamine.

Serotonin and dopamine facilitate communication within the brain and between the brain and the rest of the central nervous system. They send chemical messages that help regulate your mood, prep your brain for sleep, and so much more. With insufficient levels of these neurotransmitters, your mental health is precarious at best. In short, you need certain aminos and their sidekick vitamins and minerals so that you can produce neurotransmitters that help maintain your mental health.

There are more than several amino acids essential for proper brain function and good emotional health. And we're going to talk about all of them. But I just want to make a quick not here first: Unlike vitamins and minerals that slowly build their levels in your system over days or weeks, amino acids start healing symptoms of depression and anxiety almost immediately. Sounds good, eh?

So, what aminos do you need to battle your symptoms of depression and anxiety?

Here's a complete list:

Tryptophan

Tryptophan can be a key player in the presence or absence of symptoms associated with depression and anxiety. Without enough tryptophan, you're at an increased risk for developing these mental health conditions. That's because low levels of tryptophan reduce serotonin activity in the brain.

So, if you increase the amount of tryptophan in your bloodstream – from supplementation and certain foods that you eat – you can treat symptoms of depression and anxiety and begin to heal. It's true. Tryptophan's ability to boost serotonin in the brain and lift symptoms of depression are well documented in clinical scientific research.

But how exactly does tryptophan help to increase serotonin levels? Well, tryptophan changes into 5-HTP, which then converts into serotonin (Ross, Jullia, The Mood Cure, p. 26). Unfortunately, however, there are things that can interfere with the process of tryptophan converting into 5-HTP.

These include:

- Low levels of tryptophan in your diet, which is common – especially in vegetarians or those who don't eat much meat or poultry and in those who eat low-calorie diets or skip meals.
- Chemicals in your food such as caffeine, alcohol, or the artificial sweetener aspartame

- Too little sunlight
- Too little exercise
- Extreme stress – because elevated stress hormones suppress tryptophan levels in the blood stream.
- A genetic tendency to underproduce serotonin, which can be aggravated by all of the above

There are other reasons that you may not get enough tryptophan in your diet.

For one, tryptophan is the least abundant amino in protein. And it's carried into the brain by transport system that prioritizes other amino acids. So basically, tryptophan gets crowded out, keeping it from passing over into the brain.

But there are ways to increase the transfer of tryptophan into the brain. For example, when you eat turkey with a carb liked mashed potatoes, the body produces insulin, which diverts other amino acids to your muscles but leaves tryptophan untouched. As a result, tryptophan can cruise into your brain. You can also take tryptophan with fruit juice, so it is more likely to cross the blood brain barrier. That's because the carbs in fruit juice signal insulin release, and insulin then carries the tryptophan across the barrier, promoting its absorption. You could also have hummus with whole wheat pita bread, for example, to speed up this transfer.

Many people simply don't get enough tryptophan in their diets because they've increased their consumption of grain-based carbohydrates like bread, pasta, corn, cookies, and so on. So, it's a good idea to cut back on these foods and eat several 4-ounce servings of protein each day in the form of meat, dairy, eggs, and soy products.

Some of the best sources of tryptophan include:

- Turkey
- Chicken
- Beef
- Pork
- Fish
- Cheese
- Eggs
- Milk
- Beans
- Soy Products
- Chickpeas

Vegetarians and vegans are especially prone to having depression caused by low levels of tryptophan. That's because, as you can see, many of the best sources of tryptophan are meats, poultry, and fish.

But some great sources of tryptophan for vegetarians and vegans include:

- Nutritional Yeast
- Almonds
- Seeds

- Bananas
- Pumpkin Seeds
- Spinach
- Tofu
- Edamame
- Chickpeas
- Walnuts
- Potatoes
- Cauliflower
-

There are some other things to consider when you're working to increase your tryptophan intake and absorption. For instance, if you don't eat enough healthy fat, you may not be getting enough tryptophan. Increasing fat intake increases tryptophan uptake in the brain.

It's also important to remember that the Standard American Diet lacks many important vitamins and minerals, some of which are needed to convert tryptophan into 5-HTP and then serotonin. You need calcium, magnesium, vitamin D, and B vitamins, to facilitate the conversion of tryptophan into serotonin.

Of special note: if you are deficient in niacin, any tryptophan you do get into your bloodstream will be converted to niacin rather than serotonin. So, that's just one more reason that it's wise to take a B Complex vitamin daily. It will give you B6 and Niacin and thereby allow the tryptophan to make serotonin.

Tyrosine

Oftentimes, people with depression have low levels of epinephrine in their systems. Fortunately, the amino acid *tyrosine* can raise these levels, as it's converted into epinephrine. The body also uses tyrosine to make dopamine and adrenaline. Therefore, tyrosine can play a substantial role in lifting symptoms of depression.

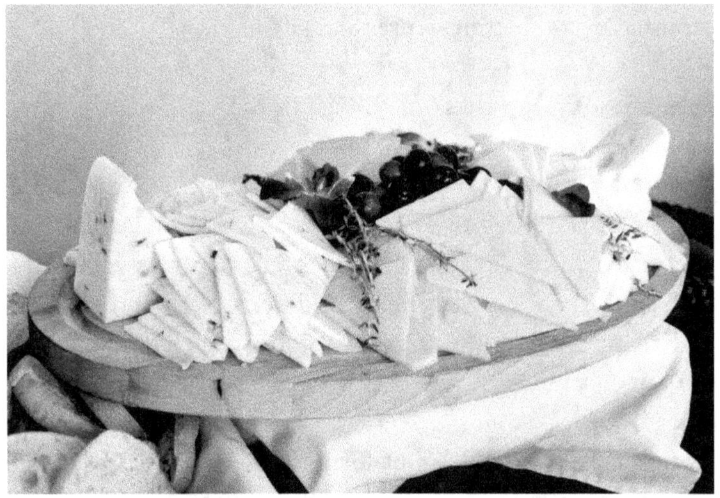

Tyrosine is mostly found in meats and cheeses.

Of note: It's important to note that tyrosine supplementation is not safe for everyone and can lead to racing thoughts, irritability, and insomnia. So, ***please*** check with your doctor before taking tyrosine in supplement form.

Phenylalanine

Phenylalanine is another amino that you need to fight off

depression. And it actually does double duty by helping your system combat stress. As you know (because I keep on repeating it), prolonged, elevated stress levels can lead to depression.

There are two forms of phenylalanine. Together, they are referred to as DLPA. Both forms help boost endorphins, which are hormones secreted within the nervous system that are essential in combatting depression and anxiety.

Here are some specifics on DLPA:

The first, **L-phenylalanine** (LPA) is one of the 15 or more base aminos needed to form endorphins and one of the five needed to form enkephalin, which are peptides related to endorphins. LPA raises energy and decreases depression by increasing stimulating neurotransmitters, such as dopamine, norepinephrine, and epinephrine or adrenaline.

Additionally, L-phenylalanine forms PEA or phenylethylamine, another energizing brain chemical that may be responsible for feelings of euphoria. Low PEA is routinely associated with depression. LPA increases levels of PEA.

So, in short, LPA helps increase dopamine, norepinephrine, epinephrine, and PEA – all of which you need to prevent and heal from depression and anxiety.

The second component of DLPA is **D-phenylalanine** (DPA). It's like the mirror image of L-phenylalanine, but it's even more potent when it comes to boosting endorphins.

Wrap Up

As explained earlier, you could have some difficulty getting certain amino acids through the foods that you eat. And therefore, you may benefit from taking supplements.

Of the aminos mentioned in this chapter, **tryptophan** and **tyrosine** play the biggest roles in treating symptoms of depression. But some people benefit more from tryptophan whereas others benefit more from tyrosine.

How do you know which one is right for you?

Well, depression presents in different ways with different symptoms.

Symptoms indicative of a tryptophan deficiency include:

- Sleeplessness
- Anxiety
- Irritability
- Nervous depression
-

And those indicative of a tyrosine deficiency include:

- Lethargy
- Fatigue
- Sleeping too much
- Feelings of immobility

So, based on your symptoms, you may want to start with either tryptophan or tyrosine supplementation. And always start with the lowest possible dose after consulting with your health care provider. You can increase your dose and add other aminos once you see how well you're doing with either tryptophan or tyrosine.

That's a wrap on the vitamins, minerals, omegas, and aminos that you need to stave off and heal from depression and anxiety. I'll see you in the next chapter

3

Balancing Blood Sugar for Mental Health

Introduction

I'm going to get straight to the pointe here: you can't have good mental health if you don't have balanced blood sugar. So, you will need to eat in a way that helps stabilize your blood sugar if you want to fight off symptoms of depression and anxiety. In this chapter, I'm going to share all the information you need to do just that.

So, let's face it, the most common foods in the Standard American Diet (SAD) combine to make the perfect concoction for all kinds of illness – and that includes mental illness. Some of the worst offenders in this diet are highly processed foods full of refined sugar and saturated fats, among other unhealthy things. And these kinds of foods can leave your blood sugar all out of whack.

Unfortunately, when you're dealing with depression and anxiety, you often crave and cave into eating comfort foods. That's because these foods give you a quick dopamine hit, which you crave. And need I even say it? These foods are often full of the refined sugar and saturated fats mentioned above. A big bowl of pasta. Pizza. French Fries. Bread. Chocolate chip cookies. Potato chips. Ice cream.

With that said, I'm now going to share some information that hopefully will inspire you to put the brakes on eating these kinds of foods.

Unbalanced blood sugar

Your blood sugar levels fluctuate throughout the day based on what you're eating and doing. That's normal. But it's important to keep them within a reasonable range.

Whether it's too high (hyperglycemia) or too low (hypo-glycemia), blood sugar levels play a huge role in both your physical and… yes… your mental health.

But how do you know when it's out of balance? Well, there are many signs. I'll start with those that are easy to recognize.

Common signs and symptoms of unbalanced blood sugar include:

- Feeling "hangry" – or agitated and hungry
- Crashing after meals
- Sweating
- Shaking
- Feeling tired and fatigued

• Feeling confused

In his book *The Depression Cure*, Stephen Ilardi lists illnesses and medical conditions that can trigger depression and anxiety. And one of these is diabetes, which involves unbalanced blood sugar. Others conditions that cause depression and anxiety include hypothyroidism, hormonal imbalances, and malnutrition.

You may be thinking that blood sugar is not an issue for you if you don't have diabetes. Many times, I've heard people say: "Oh no. Blood sugar is not a problem for me. I don't have diabetes." And with that, I can only guess that they're thinking they can keep on eating all the refined carbs I want.

But here's the thing… you don't need to have diabetes to have unbalanced blood sugar and to suffer from the negative physical and mental health consequences of that. When you have blood sugar levels that spike up high and/or sink down low, you'll see that your overall health – *including* your mental health – really suffers.

As is often the case in life, it's not really clear which comes first – the chicken or the egg. Does continuously unbalanced blood sugar cause depression? Or does depression cause unbalanced blood sugar because depressed people often resort to carb-loaded comfort foods?

I can't say for sure, and I think it could go either way. Regardless, unbalanced blood sugar is associated with depression and anxiety. And balanced blood sugar is not.

Balanced blood sugar:

- Prevents you from feeling hangry – or irritable because you're hungry.
- Prevents excessive hunger.
- Helps stabilize your energy levels.
- Helps you maintain focus.
- Balances your hormones.
- Promotes weight loss.

And here's the big one…

- ***Encourages overall feelings of well-being and better mental health.***

Sounds pretty great, eh?

With unbalanced blood sugar, you waffle between hyper-glycemia and hypoglycemia. And your mood can spike and crash as you experience these blood sugar highs and lows.

Causes of Unbalanced Blood Sugar

Hyperglycemia is **elevated blood sugar** that results from having **too little insulin** in the bloodstream.

Causes of hyperglycemia include:

- **Elevated** levels of stress hormones such as **adrenaline and cortisol**, which interfere with your body's ability to use insulin appropriately and therefore leaves too much glucose in the blood.
- Limited **physical activity**.
- Consumption of **processed foods** full of **simple carbs** and **fat**.
- **Frequent snacking** between meals.

Symptoms of hyperglycemia include:

- Increased thirst
- Dry mouth
- Frequent urination
- Fatigue
- Blurred vision
- Stomach pain, nausea, vomiting

Hypoglycemia is **low blood sugar** that results from having **excessive insulin** in the bloodstream. The more sugar and simple carbohydrates you eat, the more insulin you release. And this can lead to hypoglycemic episode of low blood glucose.

Causes of hypoglycemia include:

- **Fasting** for 8 or more hours.
- Certain **medications**, such as aspirin, birth control pills, steroids, blood pressure medication, and some antibiotics.
- Excessive intense **physical activity**.
- Consumption of **"naked carbs,"** which are carb heavy foods with very little fiber and protein.
- Excessive consumption of **alcohol**.
- Diminished levels of cortisol, growth hormone, glucagon, and epinephrine.

Symptoms of hypoglycemia include:

- Headaches
- Irritability
- Tiredness
- Dizziness
- Confusion
- Forgetfulness
- Lack of coordination
- Inability to focus
- Anti-social behavior
- Nervousness
- Cold sweats
- Tremors
- Rapid pulse
- Pounding heart
- Shortness of breath
- Sleepiness after meals or in the late afternoon
- Anxiety

And here's a big one... Hypoglycemia may instigate metabolic changes in your brain and nervous system that mess with your mood, change your behavior, and leave you feeling emotionally unstable.

Wow! Right?

In *Depression-Free, Naturally*, Joan Mathews Larson clarifies the symptoms of hypoglycemia that may be associated with depression and/or anxiety:

- **Unstable moods**, which result from fluctuating blood sugar levels.
- **Nightmares or other sleep disturbances**, which are indicative of low levels of vitamin B6, a nutrient used up in metabolizing refined sugars.

- **Insomnia**, characterized by difficulty falling asleep and waking during the night.
- **Nervous exhaustion**, which involves feeling on the edge and overly fatigued.
- **Indecision**, which we talked about in the Mindset Module.

I'm sure you can see that many of those are the very same in a list of the symptoms associated with depression and anxiety.

How to Balance Your Blood Sugar

The big question now is: How can you balance your blood sugar?

Let's talk about this because when you do have balanced blood sugar, you'll be healthier – both mentally and physically.

Obviously, blood sugar levels have a lot to do with what you eat.

But certain lifestyle habits factor in as well.

To **prevent hyperglycemia** you can:

- **Eat fewer refined carbs**, because refined carbs and sugar cause your blood sugar to spike and then crash. These fluctuations are the hallmark of unbalanced blood sugar. And diets high in these types of foods have been linked to increased appetite, weight gain, type 2 diabetes, high blood pressure, hyperactivity, and, yes, mood disorders.

- **Don't eat naked carbs**. This simply means that you shouldn't eat a carb on its own without also eating some fiber, protein, and healthy fat. So, it's better to eat an apple with a little peanut butter than it is to just eat an apple.

- **Eat more fruits and vegetables**. Good old fruits and veggies. They contain fiber that helps slow the digestion process, and this helps to prevent blood sugar spikes.
- **Avoid eating late at night**. This can increase your insulin levels and affect how your cells respond to insulin or cause insulin resistance. And insulin levels already spike during the night, even when you don't eat a thing.
- **Regularly engage in physical activity**. The goal is to get in at least 30 minutes of physical activity five times a week. Exercise triggers the production of insulin receptors. And

your body can process blood glucose and build stronger cells when you have more of these receptors. Once you build these receptors, you have them for life.

- **Sleep for 6 to 8 hours every night**. Getting less than 6 hours of sleep a night has been shown to make a person's cells less sensitive to insulin. And increased insulin resistance in cells significantly increases blood sugar levels.

And to **prevent hypoglycemia,** you can:

- **Don't skip meals**, because this puts you at risk of having low blood sugar levels.

- **Eat small meals every 3 to 4 hours throughout the day instead of eating 3 large meals**, because a steady intake of foods keeps your blood sugar levels steady as well.

- **Increase calories if you increase physical activity**, because your body needs more energy when you're active. And if you don't eat enough, your blood sugar levels may plummet.
- **Exercise regularly but not excessively**. When you exercise, your body needs more glucose. If you exercise too much, you will deplete your glucose stores and experience hypoglycemia.
- **Consume an adequate amount of complex carbo-hydrates**. Forty-five to sixty-five percent of your daily intake should be complex carbohydrates. And the best

sources of complex carbs are fruits and vegetables. It takes more time to digest complex carbs, and the lengthy process helps you avoid blood sugar spikes and crashes. But be somewhat mindful of the amount of bread, grains, fruits, and veggies that you eat without also eating a bit of protein or healthy fat at the same time. As a rule, you should pair high carb foods with healthy fat and protein to slow the rate at which you absorb sugar.

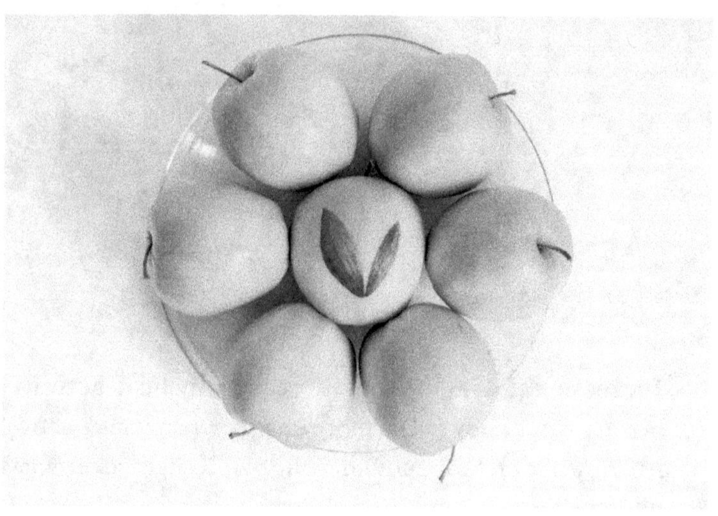

- **Eliminate or at least reduce foods full of refined and processed sugars**. I love this – the way it's stated, that is. In *The Depression Cure*, Ilardi says that "Sugar is a dangerous inflammatory villain lurking at the heart of the modern western diet" (p. 247). The average American eats eighty pounds of processed sugar each year! That's equivalent to

25 teaspoons of sugar or 400 calories each day. And these sugar-laden foods will cause your blood sugar levels to rise quickly and then crash suddenly.

- **Avoid foods high in saturated fat**, because saturated fats can aggravate symptoms of hypoglycemia by increasing inflammation.
- **Eat lean proteins**, because it takes time for protein to digest, and this lengthy process helps stabilize the absorption of glucose into the bloodstream.

- **Avoid drinking too much alcohol**, because it destabilizes blood sugar levels.
- **Choose to eat foods with a low glycemic index score**. I'll talk more about this later in the chapter.

Now I'd like to talk a little bit about balancing blood sugar with minerals and amino acids.

There are some minerals that may help balance your blood sugar.

These minerals include:

- **Chromium**, which is essential for sugar metabolism. It attaches to insulin receptors and boosts insulin activity. And it can help raise low glucose levels and lower high ones.
- **Magnesium**, which helps the body process glucose and maintain normal glucose levels. In other words, it balances your blood sugar.

And then there's also a blood-sugar balancing amino acid:

- **Glutamine** is an amino acid that may help prevent sugar cravings because it converts to glutamic acid in the brain. So, it can serve as a great alternative source of brain fuel that can prevent cravings triggered by hypoglycemia.

And it's true! There are a few spices that may help regulate blood sugar, which include:

- **Cinnamon**, which increases insulin sensitivity and decreases blood sugar.

- **Turmeric**, which helps stabilize blood sugar levels.
- **Ginger**, which helps lower blood sugar levels and regulate insulin.

The Glycemic Index

If you're going to balance your blood sugar, you have to know a little the glycemic index (GI) - a value used to assess how individual foods will affect a person's blood sugar levels.

There are low, medium, and high glycemic index foods - ranked on a number scale of 0 to 100. The lower a food's GI value, the less it affects blood sugar.

- Foods that have GI values of **55 or less** are considered **low** on the GI scale and have the least impact on blood sugar.
- Foods that have GI values of **56 to 69** are considered **medium** on the GI scale and have some impact on blood sugar.
- And foods that have GI values of **70 and above** are considered **high** on the GI scale and have a significant impact on blood sugar levels.

Foods that fall into the 70+ GI value include those with refined carbs and sugar that are digested quickly. And foods that include protein, fat, or fiber often fall into the low GI range. Aside from nutrient composition, other factors that influence where a food falls on the glycemic index include processing, cooking method, and ripeness.

It's important to note that the GI is not the same as the Glycemic Load (GL), which considers the serving size of a food when determining how it will affect blood sugar. You may want to consider both the GI and the GL have diabetes.

There are also some foods that do not contain any carbs and are not included on the GI index.

These foods include:

- Seafoods: Tuna, Salmon, Shrimp, Mackerel, Anchovies, Sardines
- Poultry: Chicken, Turkey, Duck, Goose
- Meats: Beef, Bison, Lamb, Pork

- Nuts: Almonds, Macadamia Nuts, Walnuts, Pistachios
- Seeds: Chia Seeds, Sesame Seeds, Hemp Seeds, Flax Seeds
- Oils: olive Oil, Coconut Oil, Avocado Oil, Vegetable Oil
- Certain Pastas: including Whole Grain Pasta and Semolina

And here's a quick rundown of certain foods rate that are considered high glycemic and low glycemic.

Low glycemic foods include:

- Certain Veggies: Broccoli, Cauliflower, Carrots, Spinach, Tomatoes

- Certain Fruits: Oranges, Lemons, Limes, Grapefruit, Blueberries, Strawberries, Raspberries, Blackberries
- Certain Beans: lentils, Black Beans, Chickpeas, Kidney Beans
- Certain Whole Grains: Quinoa, Oats, Barley, Buckwheat, Farro

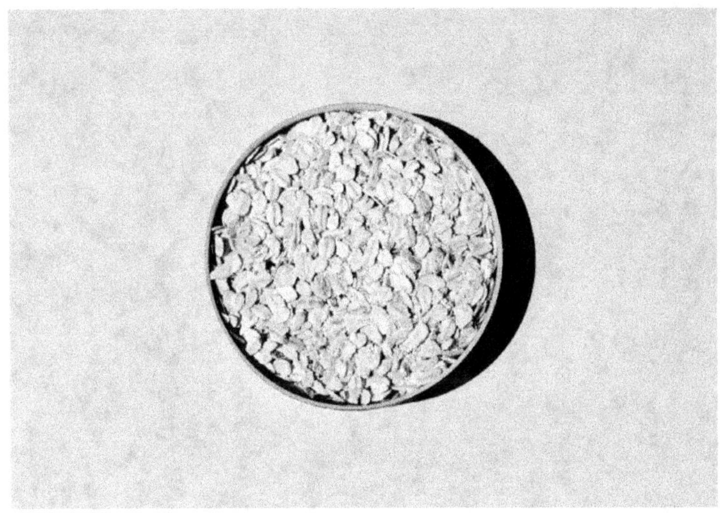

High glycemic foods include:

- Baked Goods: Doughnuts, Muffins, Croissants, Cookies, Cake
- Certain Breads: Bagels, Pita Bread, White Bread

- Certain Cereals: Instant Oats, Breakfast Cereals
- Certain Kinds of Rice: White Rice, Jasmine Rise, Arborio

- Starch Vegetables: Potatoes

Also don't forget to check out a more comprehensive list of foods with their GI ratings in the appendix of this book.

Wrap Up

That's all I have on balancing blood sugar for now. Hopefully you can see just why balanced blood sugar is so critical for anyone prone to depression and anxiety. And the good news is that balancing blood sugar is really not so hard to do. Once you get a feel for where foods fall on the glycemic index, you'll be well on your way to better mental health.

That's all I have on this topic for now. I will see you in the next chapter

4

The Connection between Gut Health and Mental Health

Introduction

When I think of the neurotransmitter serotonin, I think of the brain. More specifically, I think of serotonin being produced in the brain. I guess that's because serotonin plays such a huge role in mental health. And I associate the word mental with the mind and the mind with the brain. So, you get the idea. Seems logical enough, right?

But the thing is that I've had it all wrong. Because actually, 90 to 95 percent of serotonin is not produced in our brains!

That's right. Rather, it's produced in our gut. And more specifically, it's made in our intestines. Really! Now chew on that for a minute. The old "gut feeling" takes on a whole new meaning when you know where serotonin is produced within the body.

Most of us think that the root cause of mental illness lies within the brain. But mental health issues signal that one or more of the body systems connected with the brain are unhealthy. (Naidoo, *This Is Your Brain on Food*, p. 12). And oftentimes the **gut** plays a role in the development of depression and anxiety. With that in mind, it's easy to see that what you put into your gut really matters when it comes to mental health. The nutrients in your diet directly affect neuropeptides, neurotransmitters, and the gut microbiota (Adan et al., 2019). Your diet is a modifiable factor in your gut's composition.

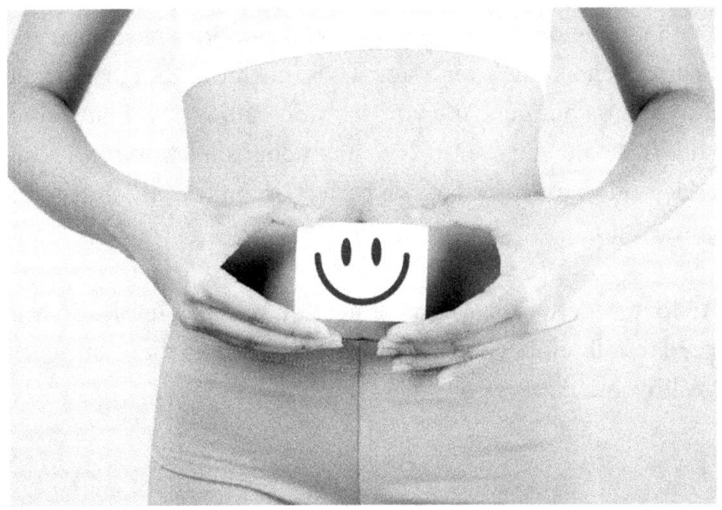

Now I want to talk a little about the **vagus nerve**, which is connected to the gut and is yet another player in the mental health game. The vagus nerve begins in the brain stem and stretches down to build a connection between the central nervous system and the gut. At the point where the vagus nerve connects to the gut, it forms threads or nerve endings that penetrate the gut wall. So, the vagus nerve plays a central role in digestion. But it also secures the connection or pathway for nerve signals to travel back and forth between the gut and the brain. And these signals travel in both directions, connecting the gut and the brain for life. The chemicals produced by your gut can travel to the brain and vice versa (Naidoo, *This Is Your Brain on Food*, p. 14).

Additionally, the foods you eat stimulate chemical development and reactions in the gut. The chemicals then travel up to the brain. And bam! There it is. Those foods end up having a huge impact on your mental health.

By the same token, your thoughts and emotions have an effect on the chemicals in your brain. Those chemicals can then travel down into your gut. And you probably know where I'm going with this. Did you ever feel anxious about something and have a "nervous" stomach? That's a perfect example of the gut-brain connection.

All that said, the gut-brain connection is real. Clearly. So, we need to talk more about what we should eat to make our guts healthy and improve our mental health.

Gut Health + Mental Health

Psychiatrist Uma Naidoo runs the Nutritional and Lifestyle Psychiatry program at Massachusetts General Hospital - the first clinic of its kind in the United States.

In her book *This is Your Brain on Food*, Dr. Naidoo admits that the relationship between nutrition and mental health may not feel intuitive. She says that we think a lot about how the food we eat affects our hearts and waistlines, but not how it affects our brains.

Naidoo also says that understanding how nutrition affects the brain is key to understanding why mental health disorders are on the rise. She notes that one in five American adults will have a diagnosable mental health condition in any given year, and that 46 percent will meet the criteria for a mental health condition at some point in their lives.

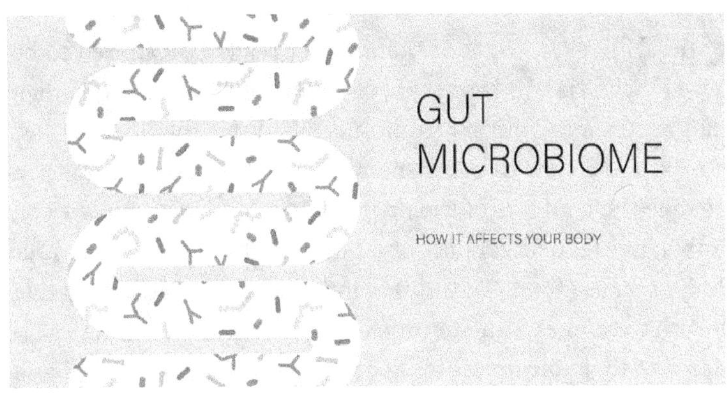

Dr. Naidoo also says: "Diet and mental health are inextricably linked, and the connection between them goes both ways: a lack of good dietary habits leads to an increase in mental health issues. And, in turn, mental health issues lead to poor eating habits.

"Until we solve nutritional problems, no amount of medication and psychotherapy is going to be able to stem the tide of mental issues in our society." (Naidoo, *This Is Your Brain on Food*, p. 4).

With that said, I'd like to share a little more detail about the gut and how those specifics impact mental health.

Some of you may already know this, but I need to make note of the fact that a giant colony of microorganisms (otherwise known as bacteria) lives in your gut. This colony is called the microbiome, and it can include up to a thousand different species of bacteria. These bacteria are loving life because the gut provides a perfect homestead and is rent free, so to speak. And none of these bacteria are freeloaders; they all have a job to do. However, some of them aren't really considered to be "good" bacteria. And you want to have more good bacteria than bad bacteria in your microbiome. Naidoo explains that diet, stress, and a slew of other mental and physical problems can change the contents of the microbiome and leave you with an imbalance of bad versus good bacteria (Naidoo, *This Is Your Brain on Food*, p. 17). And this imbalance can cause negative health outcomes – including mental health issues. There's no denying that your microbiota or the bacteria in your gut has a say in how well you respond to stress and whether or not you develop depression and anxiety (Adan et al., 2019).

We've talked a lot already about**serotonin**, which is, as you well know by now, deficient in depressed and anxious people. It plays a critical role in regulating mood and processing emotions. It also has a starring role in the gut-brain axis. And as I mentioned in the introduction, 90 to 95% of serotonin receptors are found in the gut. So again, some research has concluded thatserotonin in the brain is heavily influenced by everything that happens in and goes into the gut (Naidoo,*This Is Your Brain on Food*, p. 16). At the same time, when you have depression and anxiety, all normal and protective effects serotonin usually has on the gut are compromised as well (Naidoo,*This Is Your Brain on Food*, p. 20).

The gut also plays a significant role in the release of**corti-sol**(Naidoo,*This Is Your Brain on Food*, p. 16).When the gut is unhappy, it may either over- or under- produce cortisol. And some cortisol that isn't supposed to get to the brain makes it there anyway. Once there, it cause issues, to say the least. (Naidoo,*This Is Your Brain on Food*, p. 16). This is an interesting fact as well... Naidoo says that it takes only two hours' worth of psychological stress to completely change the bacteria in your gut. Even a tense family Christmas dinner or bad traffic can be enough to upset the balance of your microbiome. (Naidoo, *This Is Your Brain on Food*, p. 20).

And then there's**leaky gutsyndrome**? What the heck is that? Well, irregularity in your microbiome may weaken your gut's wall, which usually serves as a barrier between bacteria and your bloodstream. But with leaky gut syndrome, bacteria leak through the gut lining and into the blood. This bacterium is not supposed to be there and can cause damage throughout the body. The bacteria may even make its way up to the brain and contribute to the development of depression (Naidoo, *This Is Your Brian on Food*, p. 61). The consumption of highly processed foods has been linked to increased permeability of the intestinal barrier – in other words, to leaky gut syndrome (Grajek et al., 2022).

Then there's this…

Bowel disorders such as **irritable bowel syndrome (IBS)** and **irritable bowel disorder (IBD)** have been associated with changes in mood. And research suggests that these mood shifts result from changes in the microbiome's bacteria that accompany the development of IBS and IBD. It's really a vicious cycle.

I want to put a little emphasis on the connection between **gut health** and **anxiety**. Because if you suffer from anxiety, you may want to put a little extra effort into healing your gut. Because the gut-brain connection plays a very important role in both the development and healing of anxiety (Naidoo, *This Is Your Brain on Food*, p. 59).

It all begins with the amygdala, which is a part of the brain that regulates stress and fear responses. And, perhaps not too surprisingly, this tiny almond-shaped mass (the amygdala that is) plays a major role in the development of anxiety. In fact, the amygdala is actually even larger and more active in people suffering from anxiety. Naidoo explains that there is a strong connection between the microbiome and the amygdala. So strong, in fact, that some researchers believe you should focus on healing the microbiome to stabilize the amygdala and diminish symptoms of anxiety beforeyoutry any other form of treatment – including medication.

Studies have shown that people with generalized anxiety disorder (GAD) have very different gut bacteria than those who don't suffer from GAD. The microbiome bacteria in those with GAD were both sparser and less diverse than those in healthy individuals. More specifically, bacteria that produce the short-chain fatty acids present in a healthy gut were scarce. And there was an overgrowth of so-called "bad" bacteria in the microbiomes of those diagnosed with GAD (Naidoo, *This Is Your Brain on Food*, p. 60)

Not so coincidentally, up to 60 % of people with anxiety also have IBS (Naidoo, *This Is Your Brain on Food*, p. 62). It's part of the whole nervous stomach scenario. Regions in the brain related to emotions and pain management don't function as well in IBS patients as they do in most individuals. And guess what… these brain abnormalities are similar to those seen in patients with an anxiety disorder (Naidoo, *This Is Your Brain on Food*, p. 61). And on and on it goes..

But the biggest takeaway from all this is that you really can improve both your mental and physical health by taking steps to heal the gut. So, let's talk about what those steps might be.

Probiotics and Prebiotics and Fiber

Again, anyone suffering with depression and/or anxiety can benefit from having more good bacteria in their gut. If normal gut bacteria are not present, its absence negatively impacts the production of neurotransmitters such as dopamine, serotonin, glutamate, and gamma aminobutyric acid (GABA).

But how can you get more good bacteria into your gut?

Probiotics and prebiotics offer a quick fix for a messed-up microbiome.

Yep, ***probiotics*** help increase the number of good or beneficial bacteria in the microbiome so that they outnumber the bad. Some psychiatrists even include probiotics in their patients' psychiatric medication treatment plans because they believe strongly in probiotics' ability to help lower levels of depression and anxiety (Naidoo, *This Is Your Brain on Food*, p. 18). The effects of probiotics on mental status have been linked with information transmission between the gut and the central nervous system via the vagus nerve (Grajek et al., 2022).

Probiotic supplements and probiotic-rich foods contain live bacteria that benefit your physical and mental health. Some research has even indicated that lactobacillus, a single bacterium commonly found in live cultures in yogurt, may help reverse depression. (Naidoo, *This Is Your Brain on Food*, p. 32) Lactobacillus is also found in many probiotic supplements.

*Then there are **prebiotics**,* which are also important for improving gut health. Good bacteria in the microbiome like to feast on prebiotics, which are types of fiber that humans cannot digest. Naidoo explains that probiotics are more effective when they have prebiotic foods available in the gut to digest (Naidoo, This Is Your Brain on Food, p. 32).

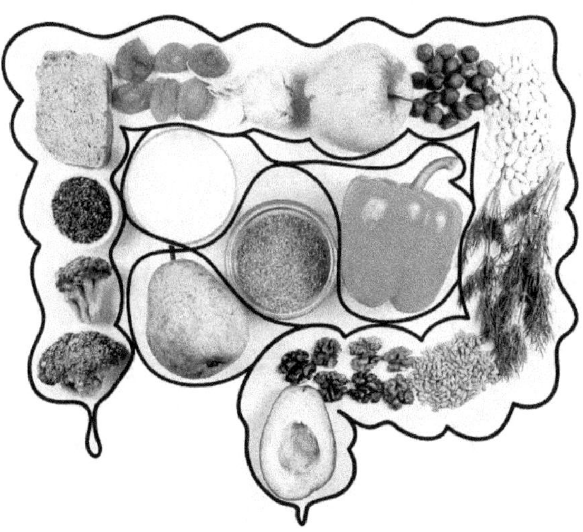

What's the best way to get more probiotics and prebiotics into your system? I'm going to give you a quick rundown of different sources.

So yes, both probiotics and prebiotics are available in supplements.

But it's always preferable to get these healthy bacteria through dietary sources whenever possible.

Dr. Uma Naidoo says that excellent sources of probiotics include:

- Yogurt with active cultures (but avoid the ones with high added sugar)
- Tempah
- Miso
- Natto (fermented soybean products)
- Sauerkraut
- Fermented Veggies such as Carrots, Cauliflower, Green Beans, Radishes, and Broccoli
- Kefir
- Kimchi
- Kombucha
- Apple Cider Vinegar
- Buttermilk
- Select Cheeses such as Cheddar, Mozzarella, and Gouda.

Generally speaking, you should look for aged, fermented, and cultured foods.

Naidoo says that excellent sources of **prebiotics** include:

- Oats
- Bananas
- Berries
- Garlic
- Onion
- Dandelion greens
- Asparagus
- Jerusalem artichokes
- Beans and other Legumes
- Leeks

(Naidoo, *This Is Your Brain on Food*, p. 33)

You can also simply get the prebiotics you need by eating a healthy dose of fresh fruits and vegetables that are full of fiber.

That said, let's talk about **fiber.**

Dietary fiber decreases inflammation throughout the body – and this includes the brain. So, you've probably heard this before, but it's just excellent advice and so I'm going to say it again. ***Eat more fiber!***

More specifically, you should look into eating *fermentable* fiber.

When dietary fiber can be broken down by bacteria, it's fermentable fiber. And fermentable dietary fiber promotes the growth of good gut bacteria, which then sets off brain and nerve signals that may alleviate symptoms anxiety and depression (Naidoo, *This Is Your Brain on Food*, p. 69).

Good sources of fermentable fiber include:

- Beans
- Brown Rice
- Berries
- Bran
- Baked Potatoes with the skin on
- Pears
- Apples
- Bananas
- Broccoli
- Brussels Sprouts
- Carrots

- Artichokes
- Almonds
- Walnuts
- Amaranth
- Oats
- Buckwheat

Quick note: Naidoo says that she has had patients who start taking prebiotics and probiotics who then feel better in *just two to three weeks*. This is pretty darn quick in the world of treatments for depression and anxiety!

Wrap Up

I hope you can see why it's so important to heal your gut when you're working to overcome depression and anxiety. It's the step you must take to seal the deal so to speak. Because without a healthy gut, you really can't absorb the nutrients you need for better mental health. And your efforts to balance your blood sugar won't really pay off either until you take that final step to heal your microbiome.

5

Meals & Snacks for Better Mental Health

T his is going to be a real short chapter, but it's an important one.

I know that all the information shared in this is a lot to absorb. And you might be wondering how you can pull all this information together to get the nutrition you need for better mental health. I understand!

So, I wanted to a few snack and meal ideas that will help you do just that. They're simple and easy. And the list could go on forever. But this short list will give you just enough inspiration to get you started.

Breakfast

- Eggs and whole grain toast with a side of mixed berries
- Steel-cut oatmeal with strawberries and thinly sliced almonds

- Greek yogurt with blackberries and chia seeds
- Overnight oats mixed with a dab of peanut butter and topped with a sliced banana
- An omelet filled with lightly sauteed veggies and served with a side of multi-grain toast
- Cottage cheese with mandarin oranges and sliced almonds

Lunch

- Salad with rotisserie chicken, cannellini beans, red peppers, cucumbers, and olive oil and vinegar dressingLentil, kidney bean, and quinoa soup
- A turkey and cheese sandwich with lettuce and tomato served on a whole grain but and with a side of carrots and hummus

- Tuna salad served with lettuce in a whole grain pita and a side of pickled veggies
- Cauliflower crust pizza topped with sauteed veggies, low-sugar pasta sauce, and fresh mozzarella
- Quesadilla with chicken, black beans, and cheese served with a side of corn and pepper salad

Dinner

- Grilled chicken, whole-wheat pasta, chopped tomato, and mozzarella cheese
- Salmon, sweet potato, and broccoli
- Sauteed teriyaki tofu and grilled veggies served over brown rice with an orange on the side
- Broiled shrimp with rice noodles tossed in light sesame oil and served with a side of Bok choy
- Vegetarian black bean burgers served on a multi-grain bun and served with a side of steamed string beans and carrot sticks
- Turkey meatloaf served with brussels sprouts and parsnip mash on the side

Snacks

- Avocado with whole wheat toast
- Apple with cheese cubes
- No sugar peanut butter and banana
- Hummus, carrot sticks, and almond crackers
- Almond butter on celery sticks with a sprinkle of raisins on top
- Greek yogurt and fruit smoothies

Mediterranean Diet

I'd also like to talk a minute about the Mediterranean diet, which is a plant-based diet incorporating the eating habits of people who live in countries bordering the Mediterranean Sea. It provides loads of health benefits – including mental health benefits. That's because the Mediterranean diet can provide all the nutrients you need, balance your blood sugar, and heal your gut so that you can fight off depression and anxiety and generally improve your mental health. In fact, numerous research studies have concluded that this diet reduces the risk of depression (Adan et al., 2019) And one study determined that participants who followed the Mediterranean diet for 12 weeks (about 3 months) significantly improved their mood, alleviated mental stress, and reduced their symptoms of anxiety (Grajek et al., 2022). So, it's worth looking into the specifics of this diet. It's easy to follow and the overall health benefits of following this type of eating pattern are too many to count.

6

Conclusion

I genuinely hope that the information shared in this book helps you along on your journey to better mental health. I know that it can.

And trust me, I've seen this happen time and again. If you change the way you eat to get the nutrients you need, balance your blood sugar, and heal your gut, you will see a tremendous improvement in your mental health. You can fight off symptoms of depression and anxiety and live a fuller life. Just use this book as your guide and take it one step at a time. You will get there.

Cheers to your mental health! You've got this one

7

Resources

Aadan, Roger A.H. van der Beek, Eline M., Buitelaar, Jan K., Cryan, John F., Hebebrand, Johannes, Higgs, Suzanne, Schellekens, Harriet, Dickson, Suzanne L. (2019). Nutritional psychiatry: Towards improving mental health by what you eat. European Neuropsychopharmacology, 29 (12), 1321-1332, https://doi.org/10.1016/j.euroneuro.2019.10.011.

Ajmera, R., MS, RD, & Kubala, J., MS, RD (2023, October 27). *Glycemic Index: What It Is and How to Use It.* Healthline. Retrieved June 9, 2024, from https://www.healthline.com/nutrition/glycemic-index

Charleson, K., & Wood, K., MD (2024, January 17). *Hypoglycemia vs. Hyperglycemia.* Verywell Health. Retrieved June 9, 2024, from https://www.verywellhealth.com/hypoglycemia-vs-hyperglycemia-5179943

Grajek, M., Krupa-Kotara, K., Białek-Dratwa, A., Sobczyk, K.,

Grot, M., Kowalski, O., & Staśkiewicz, W. (2022). Nutrition and mental health: A review of current knowledge about the impact of diet on mental health. *Frontiers in Nutrition, 9,* https://doi.org/10.3389/fnut.2022.943998

Higuera, V., & Matta, H., DO (2020, July 22). *Hyperglycemia vs. Hypoglycemia: What's the Difference?* Healthline. Retrieved June 9, 2024, from https://www.healthline.com/health/diabetes/hyperglycemia-vs-hypoglycemia

Ilardi, S. S., PhD (2009). *The Depression Cure: The 6-Step Program to Beat Depression without Drugs.* Da Capo Lifelong Books.

Mathews-Larson, J., PhD (2001). *Depression Free Naturally: Seven Weeks to Eliminating Anxiety, Despair, Fatigue, and Anger from Your Life.* Wellspring/Ballentine.

Naidoo, U. MD (2020). *This Is Your Brain On Food: An Indispensable Guide to the Surprising Foods that Fight Depression, Anxiety, PTSD, OCD, ADHD, and More.* Little, Brown Spark.

Ross, J. (2003). *The Mood Cure: The 4-Step Program to Take Charge of Your Emotions - Today.* Penguin Life.

Rucklidge, J. J., Johnstone, J. M., & Kaplan, B. J. (2021). Nutrition Provides the Essential Foundation for Optimizing Mental Health. *Evidence-Based Practice in Child and Adolescent Mental Health, 6*(1), 131–154. https://doi.org/10.1080/23794925.2021.1875342

8

Appendix

The Glycemic Index

Low GI - < or = 55

- Apple = 40
- Banana = 47
- Grapes = 43
- Strawberries = 40
- Mango = 51
- Orange = 48
- Grapefruit = 25
- Pineapple = 51
- Carrots, raw = 35
- Corn, sweet = 55
- Lima Beans = 32
- Potato = 54
- Chickpeas = 36

- Hummus = 6
- Lentils, canned = 42
- Black Beans = 30
- Cashews = 25
- Skim Milk = 32
- Yogurt, fruit = 41
- Brown Rice, steamed = 50
- Rice Noodles = 53
- White Pasta = 49
- White Rice, boiled = 47
- Rolled Oats = 55
- Chocolate = 40

Medium GI - 56-69

- Pineapple = 59
- Cantaloupe = 65
- Cherries = 63
- Kiwi = 58
- Peaches = 56
- Sweet Potato, boiled = 63
- Beetroot = 64
- Pumpkin = 66
- Black Bean Soup = 64
- Split Pea Soup = 60
- Bagel, white = 69
- Pancakes, homemade = 66
- Shredded Wheat Ceral = 67
- Pita Bread, white = 57
- Couscous = 65

- Brown Rice, boiled = 68
- Taco Shells = 68
- Macaroni & Cheese = 64
- Popcorn = 65
- Croissant = 67
- Shortbread Cookies = 64
- Honey = 58
- Sugar = 65

High GI - 70-100

- Watermelon = 80
- Potato, boiled = 78
- Potato, mashed = 83
- Rice Cakes, white = 82
- White Rice, boiled = 73
- White Bread = 70
- Wheat Bread = 74
- French Baguette = 95
- Rice Crackers = 87
- Pretzels = 83
- Waffles = 76
- Cheerios = 74
- Rice Chex = 89
- French Fries = 75
- Pizza, cheese = 80
- Doughnuts, cake = 76
- Graham Crackers = 74
- Jelly Beans = 80

About the Author

Hi all! I'm Anne, a nutrition education specialist, mindfulness instructor, and integrative wellness coach who specializes in helping women overcome symptoms associated with depression and anxiety. Please stop by annedeleeuw.com for more information on healing from mental health conditions through integrative nutritional therapy.

You can connect with me on:

🌐 https://annedeleeuw.com